I0410918

September 2014

BUREAU OF RECLAMATION

Availability of Information on Repayment of Water Project Construction Costs Could Be Better Promoted

GAO-14-764

September 2014

GAO Highlights

Highlights of GAO-14-764, a report to congressional requesters

BUREAU OF RECLAMATION

Availability of Information on Repayment of Water Project Construction Costs Could Be Better Promoted

Why GAO Did This Study

Since 1902, Reclamation has financed and built water projects to provide water for irrigation and various other uses in 17 western states. The costs to construct the water projects including irrigation as a project purpose—a combined total of more than $20 billion—were primarily financed by the federal government, but irrigation districts and other water users that receive project water are obligated to repay the government for their allocated share of construction costs. Reclamation typically enters into multiyear contracts with irrigation districts that establish water delivery and repayment of their share of construction costs over time.

GAO was asked to provide information on the status of irrigation repayments. This report examines (1) the extent to which Reclamation collects and reports information on construction costs and the status of repayment and (2) the extent to which irrigation districts can repay early and the implications of early repayment. GAO reviewed laws and policies; fiscal year 2012 construction cost repayment and early repayment data; and interviewed Reclamation officials and nonprobability samples of eight irrigation districts and nine individuals knowledgeable about water projects.

What GAO Recommends

GAO recommends that Reclamation better promote to the public that information on water projects' construction costs and repayment status is available. The Department of the Interior concurred with the recommendation.

View GAO-14-764. For more information, contact Steve D. Morris at (202) 512-3841 or morriss@gao.gov.

What GAO Found

The Department of the Interior's Bureau of Reclamation collects information on water project construction costs and the status of repayment by irrigation districts—entities that have entered into contracts with the agency to receive project water for irrigation purposes—but has not publicly reported repayment information since the 1980s. Reclamation's data on water project construction cost repayments indicate that, of the $6.4 billion in costs allocated to irrigation as of the end of fiscal year 2012, $1.6 billion remains outstanding. The remaining $4.8 billion has been repaid by irrigation districts or through other revenue sources or will be provided in financial assistance to the districts. Reclamation's policy is to make the statements it prepares annually on repayment available to the public upon request, but the agency does not make it readily known to the public that it prepares these statements or that they are available. GAO interviewed individuals knowledgeable of Reclamation water projects who indicated that this information would be useful for their work, such as in considering funding arrangements for the expansion of water projects; some individuals were not aware that Reclamation prepares repayment statements annually, or that the agency would make them available upon request. By more widely disseminating information to the public that construction cost and repayment data are available, Reclamation may increase interested parties' opportunities to obtain cost and repayment information. This, in turn, could further enable Congress, water users, and the public to assess past funding arrangements and enhance their ability to make informed decisions for funding potential new work, such as to expand water storage capacity.

The authority for irrigation districts—or for landholders who own or lease land for agricultural purposes within those districts—to repay their allocated share of construction costs early is limited to a small number of districts, and its use has various financial and other implications. Early repayment authority allows irrigation districts or landholders to repay their total outstanding repayment obligations in advance of the date specified in the districts' contracts. As of December 2013, 87 irrigation districts—representing about 15 percent of all districts with contracts—had authority for the district or its landholders to repay early. Of those authorized, 69 irrigation districts either repaid early, or had some landholders who repaid early, with those payments totaling more than $238.9 million. GAO found that early repayment's effect on the financial return to the federal government largely depends on whether a discount may be authorized, such as calculating the present value of the outstanding repayment obligation to determine the amount to be repaid early, and the size of that discount. If no discounts are authorized, any early repayments that occur would be worth more to the government because the repayments do not bear interest. In addition, early repayment accelerates the elimination of certain restrictions and requirements for landholders that are in place until their repayment obligation is fulfilled. For example, once landholders have fully repaid their construction cost obligations, they are no longer subject to acreage limits on the amount of land they can own or lease for agricultural purposes and irrigate with project water and may be able to receive project water on additional land.

_____ **United States Government Accountability Office**

Contents

Figures

GAO U.S. GOVERNMENT ACCOUNTABILITY OFFICE

441 G St. N.W.
Washington, DC 20548

September 8, 2014

The Honorable Peter DeFazio
Ranking Member
Committee on Natural Resources
House of Representatives

The Honorable Grace F. Napolitano
Ranking Member
Subcommittee on Water and Power
Committee on Natural Resources
House of Representatives

The Honorable Edward J. Markey
United States Senate

The Honorable Jared Huffman
House of Representatives

Since 1902, the Department of the Interior's Bureau of Reclamation has
financed and built more than 180 water projects—comprising dams,
reservoirs, canals, and other features to store and deliver water—to
provide water to various users in 17 western states. Initially, water
projects were intended to make previously arid and semiarid land
productive and were built almost solely for irrigation. Over the years,
water projects grew in size and purpose, often providing water for
irrigation, as well as hydroelectric power generation, municipal and
industrial water supplies, recreation, flood control, and fish and wildlife
enhancement, among other uses. Today, Reclamation's water projects
vary substantially in size, ranging from a 5,000-acre water project in
southeastern Idaho consisting of a single canal, to the roughly 500-mile
long Central Valley Project in California consisting of 20 dams and
reservoirs, and hundreds of miles of canals. Collectively, Reclamation's
projects provide water for about 10 million acres of farmland and nearly
31 million people. The costs to construct the water projects including
irrigation as a project purpose—a combined total of more than $20
billion—were primarily financed by the federal government, but irrigation

districts,[1] power users,[2] and municipal and industrial users (collectively called water users) that receive project water are obligated to repay the federal government for their allocated share of construction costs. Water users are also obligated to pay the government for ongoing operation and maintenance performed by Reclamation.[3]

Reclamation typically enters into multiyear contracts with water users that are agreements between the federal government and the user on the delivery of water, the repayment of construction costs, and other terms and conditions. Repayment requirements vary depending on the type of water use and contract. For example, irrigation districts with repayment contracts are generally required to repay their allocated construction costs over a period of up to 40 years, and they do not pay interest on their allocated construction costs. In contrast, power and municipal and industrial users are required to repay their allocated share of construction costs over a period of up to 40 years as well, but they are also required to pay interest that accrues on those costs over time.

As congressional authorization for new water projects slowed by the 1970s, Reclamation shifted its focus from constructing to managing water projects, including providing maintenance, repair, and modernization of existing infrastructure. Going forward, however, as population, agricultural production, and development in the West are projected to continue to increase, Reclamation may be called upon to expand existing capacity for water storage or delivery or to support additional conservation measures for fish and wildlife enhancement. For instance, severe drought conditions in California in 2014 have led some Members of Congress to call for

---

[1]In this report, we use the term "irrigation districts" to mean entities established under state law that have entered into contracts with Reclamation to receive project water for irrigation purposes, which generally encompasses water used to irrigate land primarily for the production of commercial agricultural crops or livestock.

[2]In this report, the term "power users" refers to users of Reclamation water project power generation. Such users include industrial entities, municipalities, Native American entities, military installations, water districts, power companies, and irrigation districts, among others. Since 1977, power generated by Reclamation water projects that is surplus to irrigation needs is marketed by the Department of Energy under rates set by that agency.

[3]Operation and maintenance payments are not included in the scope of this review. We previously reported on Reclamation water project operation and maintenance activities and costs; see GAO, *Bureau of Reclamation: Information on Operations and Maintenance Activities and Costs at Multipurpose Water Projects*, GAO/AIMD-00-127 (Washington, D.C.: May 31, 2000).

increasing the water storage capabilities of water projects located in the state and have highlighted the importance of effective water management across the West. There has also been congressional interest in broadly authorizing the early repayment of construction costs—that is, allowing irrigation districts to pay off their allocated construction costs before the due date specified in their contracts.[4] Unless expressly authorized in their contracts or by statute, irrigation districts are not authorized to repay their construction cost obligations early.

In this context, you asked us to provide information on the status of irrigation districts' repayments of their allocated water project construction costs. This report examines (1) the extent to which Reclamation collects and reports information on water project construction costs and the status of repayment by irrigation districts and (2) the extent to which irrigation districts can repay their allocated water project construction costs early and the implications of early repayment.

To conduct our work, we reviewed relevant laws, Reclamation policies and directives, and other Reclamation documents on water project construction cost allocation, repayment, and early repayment. We also reviewed our July 1996 report on the status of construction cost allocations and repayments at that time.[5] To determine the extent to which Reclamation collects and reports information on water project construction costs and the status of repayment by irrigation districts, we reviewed data from Reclamation's Statements of Project Construction Cost and Repayment for fiscal year 2012, the most current data available at the time of our review.[6] To examine the extent to which irrigation

---

[4]In June 2012, and again in February 2014, the Natural Resources Committee of the U.S. House of Representatives held hearings on draft legislation that would authorize irrigation districts and other water users to repay their allocated construction costs before the repayment due date specified in their contracts. The Accelerated Revenue, Repayment and Surface Water Storage Enhancement Act was introduced in the U.S. House of Representatives. H.R. 3981, 113th Cong. (2014).

[5]GAO, *Bureau of Reclamation: Information on Allocation and Repayment of Costs of Constructing Water Projects,* GAO/RCED-96-109 (Washington, D.C.: July 3, 1996).

[6]Reclamation prepares Statements of Project Construction Cost and Repayment annually for each water project that has construction costs allocated to one or more water users with repayments outstanding. The statements include data on the total construction costs for the water project; the construction costs allocated to each project purpose, including irrigation; repayment information for costs allocated to each project purpose, including the amount irrigation districts have repaid as of the end of the fiscal year; and any financial assistance granted to irrigation districts.

districts can repay water project construction costs early and the implications of early repayment, we collected data from Reclamation on irrigation districts that have authority to repay early, districts that have exercised such authority, and the amounts of early repayments through December 2013. To assess the reliability of Reclamation repayment and early repayment data, we took steps such as identifying the sources of data included in the Statements of Project Construction Cost and Repayment, which are generally tied to audited accounting records, and the agency's review process. We found the data to be sufficiently reliable for our purposes. In addition, for both objectives, we conducted interviews with knowledgeable Reclamation officials at the agency's central office in Denver, Colorado, and all five regional offices (Great Plains, Lower Colorado, Mid-Pacific, Pacific Northwest, and Upper Colorado) about issues related to the status of repayment and early repayment. We also interviewed officials from a nonprobability sample of eight irrigation districts and two landholders—who own or lease land for agricultural purposes—from five water projects located in California, Nebraska, Oregon, and Wyoming to collect information on the repayment of construction costs and related issues. We selected these irrigation districts and landholders using criteria such as the type of contracts the districts held with Reclamation, the district's status of repayment, and whether or not the districts had early repayment authority.[7] We also interviewed a nonprobability sample of nine individuals knowledgeable about Reclamation water projects and the status of repayments, early repayment authority, or both, including staff from the Congressional Research Service, Congressional Budget Office, and attorneys who have represented irrigation districts or environmental organizations. Appendix I presents a more detailed description of our objectives, scope, and methodology.

We conducted this performance audit from June 2013 to September 2014 in accordance with generally accepted government auditing standards. Those standards require that we plan and perform the audit to obtain sufficient, appropriate evidence to provide a reasonable basis for our findings and conclusions based on our audit objectives. We believe that the evidence obtained provides a reasonable basis for our findings and conclusions based on our audit objectives.

---

[7]Because we selected a nonprobability sample, the information obtained from these interviews is not generalizable to other irrigation districts or landholders, but it provides illustrative information.

Background

Reclamation has carried out its mission to manage, develop, and protect water and related resources in 17 western states since 1902. The agency has led or provided assistance in constructing most of the large dams and water diversion structures in the West for the purpose of developing water supplies for irrigation, as well as for other purposes, including hydroelectric power generation, municipal and industrial water supplies, recreation, flood control, and fish and wildlife enhancement. Reclamation is organized into five regions, with technical and policy support provided by its central office in Denver. Each regional office oversees the water projects located within its regional boundaries (see fig. 1).

Figure 1: Bureau of Reclamation Regional Boundaries

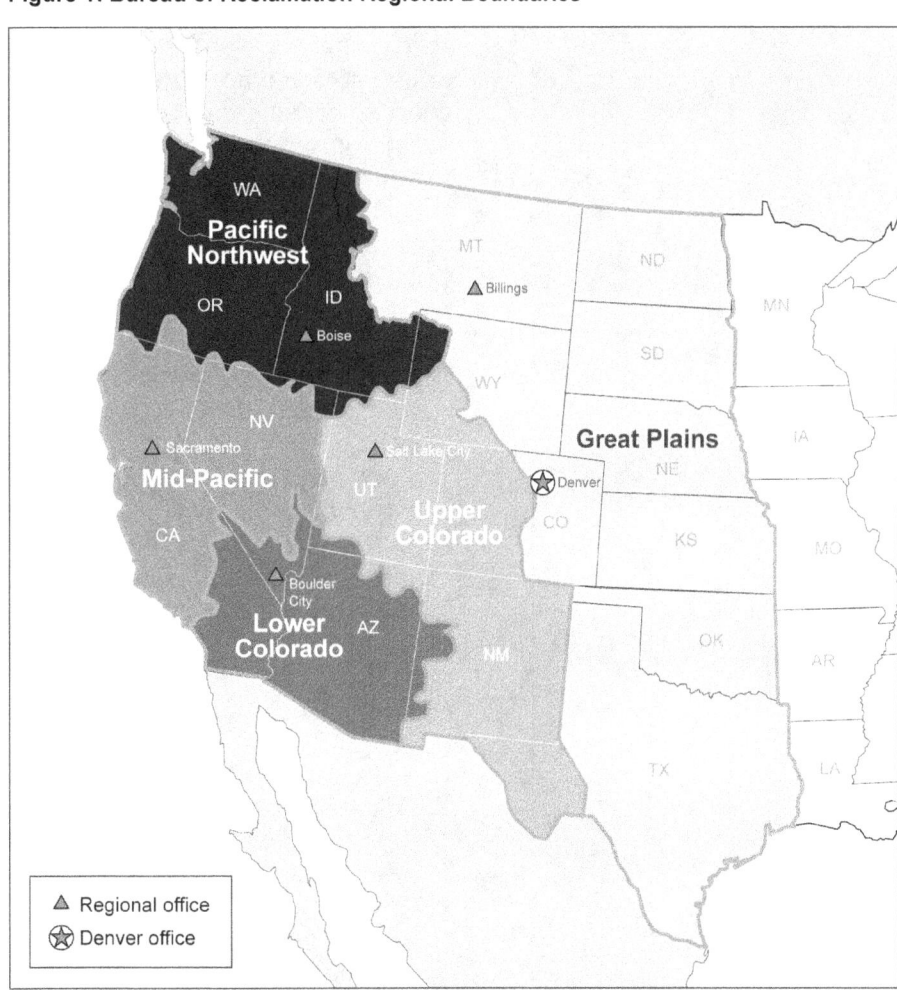

Sources: Bureau of Reclamation; Map Resources (map). | GAO-14-764

The federal statutes authorizing individual water projects and the statutes generally applicable to all water projects—known collectively as reclamation law—govern Reclamation's water projects. Reclamation law determines how the costs of constructing water projects are allocated and how repayment responsibilities are assigned among the projects' users. Cost allocation is the process of assigning an equitable share of the total cost to each use in a multipurpose project. Under reclamation law, Reclamation allocates a share of the project's total construction costs to each of the authorized project purposes based on the proportion of benefits each purpose receives from the project, and the costs allocated to each purpose are deemed to be reimbursable or nonreimbursable. Reimbursable costs are those that are to be repaid by certain water users, including irrigation districts, power, and municipal and industrial water suppliers. Nonreimbursable costs are those that are not repaid by water users and are instead generally borne by the federal government because certain project purposes are viewed by Congress as being national in scope, such as costs allocated to flood control and navigation, fish and wildlife enhancement, and recreation. At the time each water project is authorized and designed, Reclamation estimates the total construction costs and allocates these costs among the project uses. Once project construction is completed, and the actual construction costs are determined, Reclamation performs a final construction cost allocation.

The cost allocation serves as a basis for the repayment terms in water users' contracts. The amount of reimbursable costs that water users are responsible for repaying is based on the type of project purpose (see fig. 2). Power and municipal and industrial users are responsible for repaying their allocated share of the construction costs, plus the interest that accrues on those costs during construction and the repayment period. For irrigation districts, however, reclamation law does not require the districts to pay interest on the construction costs allocated to irrigation, resulting in federally subsidized financing for irrigation districts responsible for repayment. In addition, irrigation districts may receive the following two types of financial assistance in repaying their allocated construction costs:

- **Irrigation assistance.** The amount of construction costs allocated to irrigation that the Secretary of the Interior determines to be above the irrigation districts' ability to pay for a given project is repaid from other revenue sources, where available. These other revenues are primarily earned from the sale of power generated by the project (or other related projects), or from the sale of municipal and industrial water, among other revenue sources. Ability-to-pay determinations are based on Reclamation's financial analysis of a given geographic area, and determinations generally occur before construction begins on a project.[8]

- **Credits**. Credits can relieve part or all of irrigation districts' repayment obligations. Types of credits include congressionally authorized repayment reductions, or "charge-offs," and construction expenses determined to be nonreimbursable. Charge-offs are credits that are often enacted through legislation in response to special circumstances, such as a determination that the land is unproductive, or the settlement of Indian water rights claims.[9]

---

[8]Reclamation's ability-to-pay analyses include estimates of the difference in farmers' income with and without an irrigation project and involve projections of farm size, type and quantity of crops, and crop prices. The irrigation districts' ability to pay is measured in terms of the farm income available to meet the annual cost of water after all crop production, overhead, and family living expenses are recognized. In general, once the ability to pay has been determined, the irrigation districts' repayment obligation is fixed for the entire repayment term based on this determination, regardless of changes in the irrigators' profitability, unless the irrigation districts request a revision. However, Reclamation officials stated that the agency's policy is to include a provision in all new or amended repayment or water service contracts requiring that ability-to-pay determinations be reviewed every 5 years.

[9]The Omnibus Adjustment Act of 1926, for example, provided repayment relief to irrigation districts within the service areas of 21 projects by forgiving about 13 percent of all the construction costs incurred up to that time—about $17.3 million—because the Secretary of the Interior determined that the land being irrigated was nonproductive, and the act provided for a reduction of the irrigation district's repayment obligation.

Figure 2: Typical Construction Cost Repayment Obligations for Bureau of Reclamation Water Project Uses

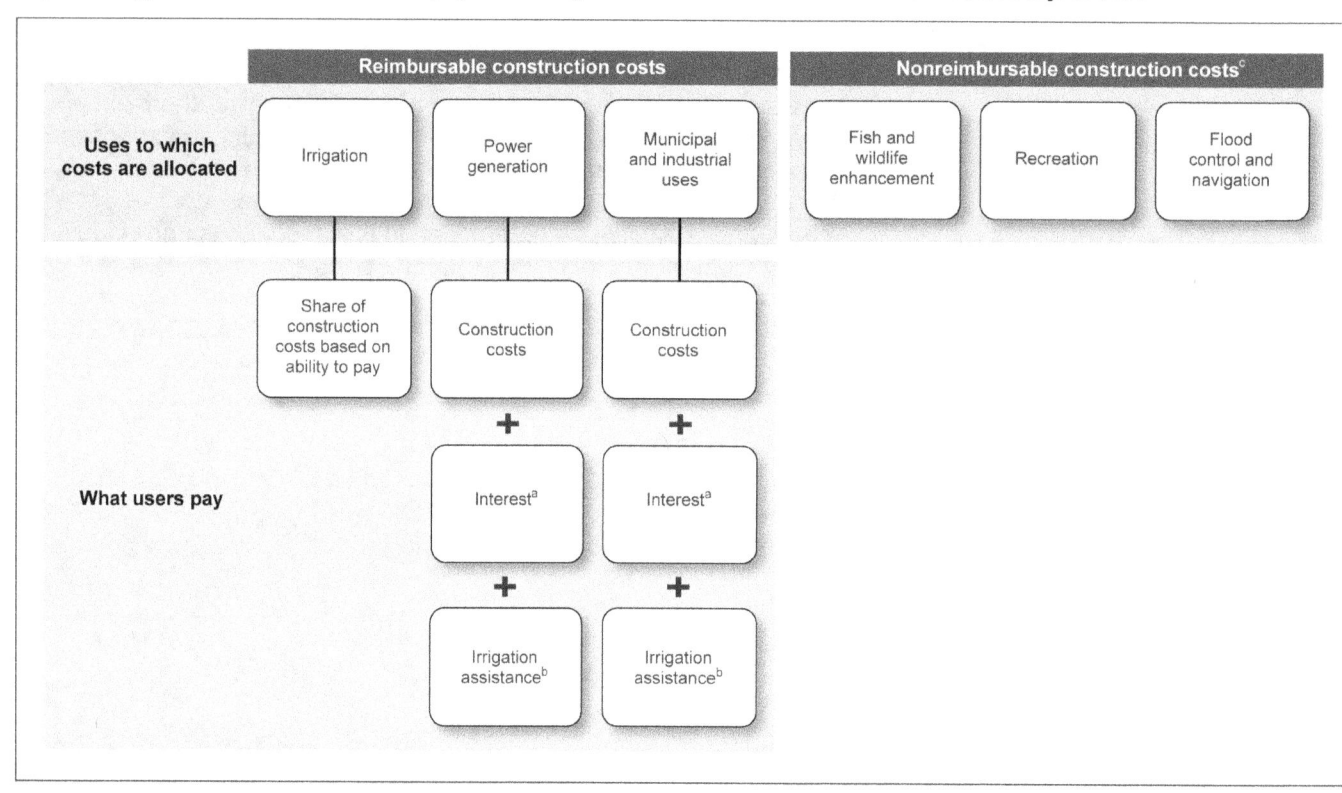

Source: GAO analysis of Bureau of Reclamation information. | GAO-14-764

[a]This includes interest during construction and the repayment period.

[b]Irrigation assistance may be provided to an irrigation district in instances when the Secretary of the Interior determines there is an amount of construction costs allocated to irrigation above the district's ability to pay for a given project, and there are revenue sources available. The amount determined to be above the irrigation district's ability to pay is repaid from other revenues, which are primarily earned from the sale of power generated by the project (or other related projects) or from the sale of municipal and industrial water, among other revenue sources. These costs do not accrue interest and are generally paid with power revenues at the end of the repayment period.

[c]Under reclamation law, nonreimbursable costs are those that are generally borne by the federal government because the project purposes are viewed as being national in scope.

To establish an agreement between the federal government and irrigation districts on the delivery of water from a project and to collect payments, Reclamation generally enters into one of the following two types of contracts with irrigation districts:

- **Repayment contracts:** Section 9(d) of the Reclamation Project Act of 1939 authorizes permanent contracts for water delivery with repayment of construction costs allocated to irrigation to be paid in fixed dollar amounts in annual or other regular increments, over a period of up to 40 years, by the irrigation district to Reclamation.[10]

- **Water service contracts:** Section 9(e) of the Reclamation Project Act of 1939 authorizes contracts to furnish water for irrigation purposes for up to 40-year periods. Reclamation generally enters into water service contracts with irrigation districts when construction of the water project has not been completed, final construction costs are uncertain, or the irrigation district does not want a permanent contract, among other reasons. By law, Reclamation must charge rates for water delivered under water service contracts that are at least sufficient to cover an appropriate share of fixed charges the Secretary of the Interior deems proper, taking into consideration the construction costs allocated to irrigation, as well as an appropriate share of annual operation and maintenance costs.[11] A water service contract can contain a provision providing for its renewal—through negotiations between Reclamation and the irrigation district—once the contract's term ends, or the contract may contain a provision allowing for its conversion to a repayment contract.[12]

---

[10]Originally, the Reclamation Act of 1902 set the repayment period at 10 years. However, because of economic difficulties faced by the irrigation districts, laws were enacted to extend this period to 20 years in 1914, and then to 40 years in 1926. Repayment periods exceeding 40 years have also been authorized by statute for specific projects. Irrigation districts with repayment contracts generally do not begin repaying their allocated share of construction costs until after a development period of up to 10 years from the time when a district first receives water from the project. The Reclamation Project Act of 1939 authorized this development period to provide irrigation districts with time to develop arid lands for farming and achieve the financial position necessary to meet the costs before beginning repayment of their share of the project's construction costs.

[11]Under water service contracts, Reclamation's rates charged for water delivered to irrigation districts are to cover an "appropriate share" of construction costs, as well as annual operation and maintenance costs, rather than the total construction costs allocated to irrigation, as under repayment contracts. According to court decisions, Reclamation has discretion in determining what constitutes an appropriate share of construction costs. See, for example, U.S. Department of the Interior, Office of Inspector General, *Central Valley Project, California: Repayment Status and Payoff*, WR-EV-BOR-0003-2012 (Washington, D.C.: March 2013), for a discussion on the share of construction costs charged to the Central Valley Project under its water service contracts.

[12]According to a Reclamation handbook, water service contracts with conversion provisions may be converted to repayment contracts if certain conditions are met.

Depending on the size of the water project, which varies substantially across projects, Reclamation may have contracts with a number of irrigation districts within that project's service area.[13] Irrigation districts then enter into separate agreements with landholders to provide project water.[14] For example, for water projects servicing a relatively small geographic area, Reclamation may have only one or two contracts with irrigation districts for that water project, which provides water to a small number of landholders. On the other hand, for water projects covering a larger area, Reclamation may have contracts with multiple irrigation districts servicing hundreds of landholders within a project.

Reclamation Collects Information on Water Project Construction Costs and the Status of Repayment by Irrigation Districts but Could Better Promote the Public Availability of This Information

Reclamation collects data on water project construction costs and the status of repayment by irrigation districts, but it has not publicly reported this information since the 1980s. Reclamation's regional offices collect repayment data annually for each water project with an outstanding construction cost repayment obligation and then compile them in Statements of Project Construction Cost and Repayment (repayment statements). These repayment statements indicate that $1.6 billion of the $6.4 billion in costs allocated to irrigation was outstanding, as of the end of fiscal year 2012. It is Reclamation policy to make the repayment statements available to the public upon request, but it could better promote to the public that it prepares repayment statements annually and that these statements are available.

[13]In some instances, Reclamation may enter into contracts directly with landholders for water service. In this report, the term "landholders" refers to individuals and legal entities such as corporations, partnerships, and tax-exempt organizations that own or lease land for agricultural purposes and receive Reclamation project water.

[14]To fulfill their obligations to Reclamation under repayment or water service contracts, irrigation districts typically collect annual payments from landholders who irrigate with project water within the districts' boundaries, and the districts then each generally submit one collective annual payment to Reclamation.

Reclamation's Data Indicate an Outstanding Repayment Obligation of $1.6 Billion Allocated to Irrigation

Reclamation's data on water project construction cost repayments indicate that, of the $6.4 billion in costs allocated to irrigation as of the end of fiscal year 2012, $1.6 billion remains outstanding. Every fiscal year, Reclamation's five regional offices collect repayment data and compile them in repayment statements for each water project that has construction costs with repayments outstanding.[15] These repayment statements include data on the total construction costs for the water project; the construction costs allocated to each project purpose, including irrigation; repayment information for costs allocated to each project purpose, including the amount irrigation districts have repaid as of the end of the fiscal year; and any financial assistance granted to irrigation districts.

Reclamation's repayment statements and other documents show that, of 130 water projects that provide water to irrigators, 54 projects have irrigation districts that have fulfilled their construction cost repayment obligations (see app. II),[16] and 76 projects have outstanding repayment obligations from irrigation districts, as of the end of fiscal year 2012 (see app. III).[17] Reclamation's repayment statements for the 76 projects show

---

[15]Reclamation policy calls for repayment statements to be prepared annually for all water projects with construction cost repayments outstanding. This policy does not apply to water projects where all water users, including irrigation districts, have repaid their construction cost allocations.

[16]Reclamation prepared repayment statements for 43 of these 54 projects in fiscal year 2012, which indicate that the total construction cost for these projects was more than $963.3 million, of which at least $350.5 million was allocated to irrigation. Reclamation did not prepare repayment statements for the other 11 projects or otherwise have construction cost and repayment information readily available. Per Reclamation policy, it is optional to prepare repayment statements for water projects where all water users, including irrigation districts, have repaid their construction cost allocations.

[17]These project numbers do not include the Klamath project in the Mid-Pacific region, which also has an outstanding repayment obligation by irrigation districts, because Reclamation has not prepared a final repayment statement for this project since fiscal year 2001. According to Reclamation officials, the repayment statement has not been finalized because they are in the process of crediting revenues from leasing land, among other things. In addition, another 31 water projects initially had construction costs allocated to irrigation, but ultimately no costs were repaid by irrigation districts pursuant to contracts with Reclamation, according to Reclamation's repayment statements, and therefore these projects are not included in our analysis.

that the total construction cost for these projects was more than $19.7 billion,[18] of which $6.4 billion was allocated to irrigation (see fig. 3).

Figure 3: Construction Cost Allocation Amounts for 76 Reclamation Water Projects with Ongoing Repayments by Irrigation Districts, as of the End of Fiscal Year 2012

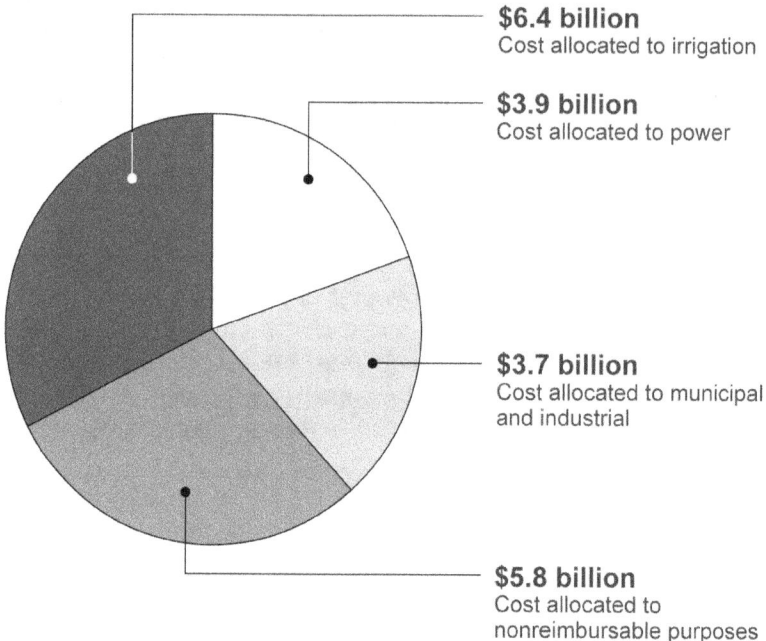

$6.4 billion
Cost allocated to irrigation

$3.9 billion
Cost allocated to power

$3.7 billion
Cost allocated to municipal and industrial

$5.8 billion
Cost allocated to nonreimbursable purposes

Source: GAO analysis of Bureau of Reclamation data. | GAO-14-764

Note: The sum of these numbers exceeds the actual total because of rounding. In addition, this figure does not include construction cost allocation amounts for the Klamath project in the Mid-Pacific region, as Reclamation has not prepared a final repayment statement for this project since fiscal year 2001 because it is in the process of crediting revenues from leasing land, among other things, according to Reclamation officials. According to a draft repayment statement prepared for the Klamath project for fiscal year 2010, the total cost of the project was approximately $121.2 million, of which $101.2 million in costs were allocated to irrigation.

According to Reclamation's repayment statements, as of the end of fiscal year 2012, of the $6.4 billion in construction costs allocated to irrigation,

---

[18]The more than $19.7 billion in construction costs includes costs that are included in Reclamation's repayment analysis or resulting repayment obligations of water users in its repayment statements, but technically may not be part of the construction cost of the project. For example, Reclamation considers deficit-funded operation and maintenance costs as a part of construction costs. When this report refers to construction costs, we are including these other costs.

the outstanding repayment obligations totaled $1.6 billion—or 25 percent—after accounting for nearly $4.8 billion in repayments made by irrigation districts, other repayments received, and financial assistance to irrigation (see table 1). Outstanding repayment obligations ranged across Reclamation's regions, from approximately $91.7 million in the Upper Colorado region to more than $1.0 billion in the Mid-Pacific region (accounting for 64 percent of the total outstanding construction costs allocated to irrigation).[19]

Table 1: Construction Costs Allocated to Irrigation and the Status of Their Repayment for 76 Reclamation Water Projects with Ongoing Repayments by Irrigation Districts, as of the End of Fiscal Year 2012

Dollars in thousands

Bureau of Reclamation region	Construction costs allocated to irrigation	Repayments received through contracts with irrigation districts	Other repayments received[a]	Financial assistance to irrigation[b]	Outstanding repayment obligations
Great Plains	$1,030,054	$155,250	$32,120	$696,553	$146,715
Lower Colorado[c]	1,155,069	60,477	42,759	848,876	202,957
Mid-Pacific[d]	1,983,386	788,272	93,510	68,298	1,033,306
Pacific Northwest	1,163,083	253,961	125,667	654,090	129,364
Upper Colorado	1,070,893	95,372	57,754	826,613	91,666
Total[e]	$6,402,485	$1,353,332	$351,812	$3,094,431	$1,604,008

Source: GAO analysis of Bureau of Reclamation data. | GAO-14-764

[a]Other repayments received include payments received from sources other than repayment from irrigation districts pursuant to contracts with Reclamation, such as miscellaneous water sales and land-use leases.

[b]Financial assistance includes irrigation assistance and credits. Irrigation assistance may be provided when the Secretary of the Interior determines that irrigation districts are unable to pay the full amount of construction costs allocated to irrigation, and responsibility for those costs is then repaid from other revenue sources, such as power, where available. Credits relieve water users from a portion of their allocated repayment obligations. Types of credits include congressionally authorized repayment reductions, or "charge-offs," and construction expenses determined to be nonreimbursable.

[c]The Lower Colorado region has one project, the Central Arizona Project, with an outstanding irrigation repayment obligation as of the end of fiscal year 2012. The Arizona Water Settlements Act, the Arizona Water Settlement Agreement, which the act ratified, and a stipulated judgment that ended multiyear litigation fixed the allocation of the project's water and repayment obligations without regard to specific water uses such as irrigation, which is the typical practice. The amounts reflected in the Central Arizona Project Statement of Project Construction Cost and Repayment for specific project purposes are inferred based on assumptions made by Reclamation officials. *See* Arizona Water Settlements Act, Pub. L. No. 108-451, tit. I, 118 Stat. 3478 (2004), the Arizona Water Settlement

[19]This percentage was calculated based on the actual (not rounded) numbers, as shown in table 1.

Agreement, and *Cent. Ariz. Water Conservation Dist. v. United States*, No. CIV 95-625, No. CIV 95-1720.

[d]Amounts presented do not include construction cost allocation amounts for the Klamath project in the Mid-Pacific region, as Reclamation has not prepared a final repayment statement for this project since fiscal year 2001 because it is in the process of crediting revenues from leasing land, among other things, according to Reclamation officials. According to a draft repayment statement prepared for the Klamath project for fiscal year 2010, $101.2 million in costs were allocated to irrigation, $9.0 million was repaid by irrigation districts, $46.2 million was repaid from other sources, $33.1 million was provided in financial assistance, and the outstanding repayment obligation was $12.8 million.

[e]Numbers may not sum to totals because of rounding. Also, the sum of repayments received, financial assistance, and outstanding repayment obligations may add up to slightly more than the construction costs allocated to irrigation because some projects expect an excess of repayment over cost, as of the end of fiscal year 2012.

Reclamation's repayment statements as of the end of fiscal year 2012 further show that, of the $1.6 billion outstanding repayment obligation for irrigation, irrigation districts are expected to repay approximately $1.1 billion through repayment or water service contracts. Of the remaining $490.4 million, approximately $287.4 million is expected to be recovered through other revenue sources, such as the sale of surplus project water for irrigation, and roughly $203.0 million is being repaid, pursuant to federal law, a settlement agreement, and stipulated judgment, by a municipal corporation that operates and maintains the Central Arizona Project.[20] Irrigation districts have repaid nearly $1.4 billion of their allocated costs primarily through repayment or water service contracts as of the end of fiscal year 2012 and, according to Reclamation officials, irrigation districts are generally current in their repayments.[21] According to Reclamation officials, across the 76 water projects with outstanding repayment obligations, Reclamation holds 72 repayment contracts for irrigation and 304 water service contracts for irrigation. We found that, across Reclamation's regions, the number of water projects with outstanding repayment obligations as of the end of fiscal year 2012 and the types of contracts vary, as described in table 2.

---

[20]The United States had entered into repayment contracts with irrigation districts for the repayment of Central Arizona Project irrigation distribution system construction costs. However, under the Central Arizona Project Settlement Act of 2004 and the Arizona Water Settlement Agreement, irrigation districts voluntarily relinquished Central Arizona Project water to which they were entitled by the terms of their contracts, among other things.

[21]The nearly $1.4 billion includes payments made pursuant to repayment and water service contracts, as well as some repayments made pursuant to rehabilitation and betterment contracts. Rehabilitation and betterment contracts are for repaying costs of maintenance for the projects, including replacement of some irrigation system infrastructure, and these costs are included in Reclamation's repayment statements.

Table 2: Bureau of Reclamation Irrigation-Related Projects and Contract Information

Bureau of Reclamation region	Total irrigation-related projects	Irrigation-related projects with outstanding repayment obligations	Repayment contracts	Water service contracts
Great Plains	39	25	12	81[a]
Lower Colorado	7	1	0[b]	0
Mid-Pacific	10	6	1	218[c]
Pacific Northwest	33	18	34[d]	5
Upper Colorado	41	26	25	0
Total	130	76	72	304

Source: Bureau of Reclamation. | GAO-14-764

Note: The information on projects is as of the end of fiscal year 2012, and the information on contracts is as of November 2013 for the Great Plains region and as of July 2014 for the other regions.

[a]This number includes 65 water service contracts with landholders.

[b]One of the seven Lower Colorado region water projects that includes irrigation—the Central Arizona Project—has ongoing repayment of construction costs allocated to irrigation, which are being repaid, pursuant to federal law, a settlement agreement, and stipulated judgment, by a municipal corporation that operates and maintains the Central Arizona Project. The United States had entered into repayment contracts with irrigation districts for the repayment of Central Arizona Project irrigation distribution system construction costs. Under the Central Arizona Project Settlement Act of 2004 and the Arizona Water Settlement Agreement, however, irrigation districts that voluntarily relinquished Central Arizona Project water to which they were entitled by the terms of their contracts received relief from their repayment obligations, among other things.

[c]Six of these contracts are San Joaquin River Settlement water service contracts with landholders. In addition, 139 of these contracts (119 of which are contracts with landholders) are Sacramento River Settlement contracts, which according to officials from the Mid-Pacific regional office, are similar to water service contracts in that they repay the same rate set for water service contracts for the Central Valley Project.

[d]Of these 34 repayment contracts, 5 are with landholders.

Reclamation Could Better Promote That Information on Water Project Construction Costs and Repayments Is Publicly Available

Reclamation has not publicly reported the information it collects on water project construction costs and repayment since the 1980s, and we found that Reclamation does not make it readily known to the public that it prepares repayment statements annually or that they are available.[22] Reclamation officials said that the purpose of the repayment statements is generally for internal management use, such as when the agency is preparing for contract negotiations, or to provide information to certain

---

[22]Reclamation publicly reported information on projects' status of repayment in *Repayment of Reclamation Projects*, which was last published in 1972, and in *Summary Statistics, Volume II, Finances and Physical Features*, last published in 1984.

power users on the amounts of irrigation assistance power may be responsible for paying. Reclamation officials told us they had considered publishing the repayment statements on the agency's website in the mid-2000s as part of an internal management review, but they decided not to do so.[23] Instead, in 2007, Reclamation developed an internal policy document on the preparation of repayment statements that states that such statements will be provided to any interested party upon request. This policy document is posted on the section of the agency's website that contains program and administrative policies that apply to Reclamation's management of its water projects. Information on the availability of the repayment statements is not otherwise posted online or made public.

We interviewed staff from legislative branch agencies and several other individuals knowledgeable about Reclamation water projects who indicated that public availability to the information contained in the repayment statements would be helpful. Some individuals we interviewed were not aware that Reclamation prepares repayment statements annually, or that the agency would make them available upon request. Several individuals we interviewed indicated that making the repayment statements directly accessible on the agency's website would be helpful and, in some cases, better inform their work. For example, a staff member from the Congressional Research Service said that to be able to respond to congressional committee requests in a timely manner, it would be helpful to have repayment information on the agency's website, similar to information posted online by Reclamation's Mid-Pacific regional office on its water rates (which are based in part on construction cost allocation and repayment information) for the Central Valley Project. In addition, some individuals noted that, as Reclamation considers modifying or expanding existing water storage capacity or delivery, Congress and others may want to assess information on how costs were allocated and how funding and repayment arrangements were established in the past to inform potential future funding arrangements. For instance, an environmental consultant told us that having repayment information

---

[23]Reclamation officials explained that the information contained in the repayment statements may not be easily understood by the public, and given the unique nature and authorizing laws for each water project, some of the cost or repayment information could be taken out of context. Reclamation officials also stated that they had encountered resistance from some irrigation districts due to concerns that other water users and the public would be able to see the status of their repayment, amounts of irrigation assistance, and other financial information in the repayment statements.

readily accessible for water projects developed in the past would help inform decisions on future funding arrangements and other policy considerations for federal, state, and other parties considering the expansion of a water project in the Pacific Northwest. A senior Reclamation official we interviewed agreed that increasing public awareness that cost allocation and repayment information is available upon request could better position the public to obtain information that could help inform their decision making on related water project issues. In addition, the official stated that there may be additional opportunities to make the public aware of its policy beyond posting the information on the policy section of its website.

According to the Office of Management and Budget's open government directive, the federal government should publish information online about what the government is doing to promote transparency, accountability, and informed participation by the public, and federal agencies should proactively use modern technology to disseminate useful information.[24] By further disseminating information to the public that cost allocation and repayment data are available through the repayment statements, Reclamation would promote transparency and potentially increase informed participation by the public.

Early Repayment Authority Is Limited, and Its Use Has Financial and Other Implications

The authority for irrigation districts, or for landholders within those districts, to repay their allocated construction costs early is limited to a small number of districts across Reclamation's water projects. Based on our analysis, early repayment affects the financial return to the federal government, and it accelerates the elimination of certain restrictions and requirements for landholders that are in place until their repayment obligations are fulfilled, among other things. Reclamation and irrigation district officials told us that early repayment may not appeal to many districts or landholders, but some districts or landholders may be incentivized to seek and exercise the authority to repay early, depending on their particular circumstances.

---

[24]Office of Management and Budget, *Open Government Directive*, M-10-06 (Washington, D.C.: Dec. 8, 2009). It defined government information as any communication or representation of knowledge such as facts, data, or opinions presented in any medium or format; see OMB Circular A-130, *Management of Federal Information Resources* (Washington, D.C.: Nov. 28, 2000).

Early Repayment Authority Is Limited to a Small Number of Irrigation Districts

The authority for irrigation districts, or for landholders within those districts, to repay their allocated water project construction costs early—that is, repay outstanding repayment obligations, either through lump-sum or accelerated payments, in advance of the date specified in the districts' contracts—is limited. Unless expressly authorized in their contracts or by statute, irrigation districts and landholders are not authorized to repay their construction cost obligations early. According to Reclamation data, of the estimated 585 irrigation districts that had repayment or water service contracts with Reclamation, as of December 2013,[25] 87 districts— or about 15 percent—had authority for the district, or for landholders within the district, to repay their construction cost obligations early. Of those 87 irrigation districts, 69 districts exercised their authority and repaid early, or had some landholders who repaid early, as of December 2013, with early repayments totaling more than $238.9 million, according to Reclamation data.

Contractual authority for early repayment is limited because only a small number of contracts that predate the Reclamation Reform Act of 1982— which prohibited new contracts after October 12, 1982, from authorizing early repayment—contain terms expressly authorizing early repayment.[26] Reclamation data indicate that of the 87 irrigation districts with early repayment authority, 55 districts had contracts that authorized landholders to repay their outstanding construction cost obligations early; these districts are located largely in the Pacific Northwest region. Some or all landholders within 39 of those 55 irrigation districts exercised this contractual authority and made early repayments totaling approximately

---

[25]According to Reclamation data, as of December 2013, an estimated 585 irrigation districts had either repayment or water service contracts, or both, with Reclamation to receive project water for irrigation purposes; this number reflects districts with outstanding repayment obligations, as well as those that have fulfilled their construction cost obligations.

[26]According to a relevant House committee report, the purpose of this prohibition was to "not permit lump-sum or accelerated payout which would inure only to the benefit of the wealthier districts and could also subvert the subsidy reduction provisions" pertaining to certain acreage and full-cost pricing limitations to which landholders are subject. H.R. Rep. No. 97-458 at 16 (1982).

$18.7 million as of December 2013,[27] according to Reclamation data (see app. IV).

In addition, we identified seven statutes enacted since 2000 that authorize some irrigation districts—or, in some cases, landholders within those districts—to repay their construction cost obligations early. Specifically, we identified 32 irrigation districts that sought and received statutory authority for early repayment by the district or landholders.[28] Our analysis of Reclamation data shows that, of those 32 irrigation districts with statutory authority, 30 districts repaid early or had some landholders within the district who repaid early, with their early repayments totaling $220.2 million, as of December 2013 (see app. IV). Twenty-two irrigation districts that receive water from the Central Valley Project and received statutory authority in 2009 comprised most of those early repayments, totaling nearly $200.1 million.

---

[27]The early repayment total of approximately $18.7 million does not include repayment information for one irrigation district. According to Reclamation data, 487 landholders in that district repaid their construction cost obligations early over a range of dates from 1940 through 2000. Reclamation did not, however, have readily available the amounts of the early repayments for that district.

[28]Four of these irrigation districts sought and received authority to have title of certain Reclamation water project assets transferred to them, and the statutes authorizing the transfers required the districts to pay specified amounts to relieve them of their outstanding repayment obligations.

Early Repayment Affects the Financial Return to the Federal Government and Accelerates the Elimination of Certain Restrictions and Requirements for Landholders

Early repayment affects the financial return to the federal government and accelerates the elimination of certain restrictions and requirements for landholders that are in place until their repayment obligations are fulfilled. While only a limited number of irrigation districts and landholders have early repayment authority, there has been consideration in Congress of expanding early repayment authority more broadly, such as to all irrigation districts.[29] Reclamation documents and officials we interviewed indicated that the agency has and would likely continue to support additional authorization for early repayment, so long as the financial return to the federal government was not negatively affected, but that the unique aspects of most water projects support authorizing early repayment on a case-by-case basis.[30]

Reclamation officials and irrigation district officials told us that early repayment may not appeal to many districts or landholders, given that their repayments are otherwise due in fixed, interest-free amounts spread over many years. In addition, some noted, the districts or landholders may not be in a financial position to repay their outstanding repayment obligations on a lump-sum or accelerated basis. On the other hand, as described above, of the 87 irrigation districts that had early repayment authority, most of the districts, or at least some of the landholders within those districts, exercised such authority and repaid their obligations early. Based on our analysis, we found that early repayment more quickly eliminates certain restrictions and requirements for a landholder, which may provide an incentive for the landholder or the district to seek and exercise early repayment authority, depending on their circumstances. Specifically, we found that early repayment has various implications for the federal government, irrigation districts, and landholders, as follows.

---

[29]In June 2012 and again in February 2014, the Natural Resources Committee of the U.S. House of Representatives held hearings on draft legislation that would authorize irrigation districts and other water users to repay their allocated construction costs before the repayment due date specified in their contracts. The Accelerated Revenue, Repayment and Surface Water Storage Enhancement Act was introduced in the U.S. House of Representatives. H.R. 3981, 113th Cong. (2014).

[30]See, for example, Statement of the Record, Bureau of Reclamation, U.S. Department of the Interior, before the Natural Resources Committee Subcommittee on Water and Power, U.S. House of Representatives, on 1. H.R. 3981, the Accelerated Revenue, Repayment, and Surface Water Storage Enhancement Act; 2. H.R. 3980, the Water Supply Permitting and Coordination Act; and 3. Discussion Draft: Legislation to Amend the Secure Water Act of 2009 (Washington, D.C.: Feb. 5, 2014).

Early Repayment Affects the Financial Return to the Federal Government

Early repayment affects the financial return to the federal government, largely depending on whether a discount may be authorized, such as calculating the present value of the outstanding repayment obligation to determine the amount to be repaid early, and the size of that discount. If no discounts are authorized, any repayments that occur earlier than the due date specified in the contract would be worth more to the government because irrigation districts' repayments do not bear interest. By receiving lump-sum or accelerated payments early for the outstanding repayment obligations, the government avoids the loss in value that would otherwise occur with repayments made over time. For example, if in 2014 an irrigation district were to make a lump-sum payment of $100,000 that would otherwise be due in annual installments through 2030 (e.g., about $5,882 per year for 17 years), the government would receive that money sooner. Looked at another way, if the irrigation district were to continue making annual repayments over time, rather than repay early, the value to the government of $100,000 paid in full after annual installments ending in 2030 would be approximately $74,220 in 2014 dollars.[31] Reclamation officials told us that in most instances where irrigation districts or landholders exercised their authority to repay early, the early repayment amounts reflected their outstanding repayment obligations, and the agency did not apply any discounts.

If early repayment authority provides a discount toward the outstanding repayment obligation, however, the value of the return to the government is reduced compared with repayment of the full outstanding amount. In recent years, a few statutes have granted certain irrigation districts a discount. For example, legislation enacted in 2009 required certain Central Valley Project irrigation districts to repay their outstanding repayment obligations early, at a discount of half the 20-year Treasury rate. This discount was intended to offset the irrigation districts' borrowing costs in obtaining loans to facilitate their early repayments, according to an attorney who represented the districts. In this example, the discount may have incentivized the irrigation districts to repay early, but it also reduced the financial return to the federal government compared with early repayment without a discount. Specifically, Reclamation data indicate that, if no discount had been applied, the early return to the government would have been $236.7 million, rather than the $200.1

---

[31]We made this calculation based on a discount rate of 3.37 percent, the 20-year Treasury rate as of March 2014.

million that was repaid based on the discount.[32] On the other hand, if such a discount had not been provided, fewer irrigation districts may have exercised their early repayment authority, and a larger discount would have resulted in a smaller return to the government.

Based on past early repayments, some irrigation districts and landholders may be motivated to repay early without a discount, but Reclamation officials told us that they believe some kind of discount would be needed to incentivize many irrigation districts to consider early repayment, were it to be authorized. Under certain scenarios, authorizing a discount could result in early repayment ultimately being worth much less to the federal government compared with repayment of the full outstanding amount. For example, in 2012, the Congressional Budget Office analyzed proposed legislation that would have expanded early repayment authority to all irrigation districts in the Central Valley Project.[33] Had it been enacted, according to that analysis, the proposed legislation would have permitted early repayments at levels approximating the present value, by applying the 20-year Treasury rate, of the irrigation districts' outstanding repayment obligations. The Congressional Budget Office estimated that if this legislation were enacted and early repayment authority were exercised by the majority of those irrigation districts, it would result in a net loss of $176 million to the government over the long-term.

Early Repayment Eliminates Acreage and Pricing Limitations for Landholders

Early repayment eliminates statutory acreage and pricing limitations for landholders sooner than if repayment is made by the due date specified in the contract. Under reclamation law, landholders who receive Reclamation project water are subject to limits on the amount of land they can own or lease for agricultural purposes and irrigate with project water, as well as the amount of land they can irrigate at subsidized rates, until they fulfill their repayment obligations.[34] Generally, until that time, landholders may not receive project water at any rate on land in excess of

---

[32]This calculation was made based on the assumption that the same number of irrigation districts would have repaid early without a discount as what occurred with the discount.

[33]Congressional Budget Office, "Cost Estimate: H.R. 1837 Sacramento-San Joaquin Valley Water Reliability Act" (Washington, D.C.: Feb. 27, 2012).

[34]Subsidized rates are any water rate other than full-cost rates, and the rate can vary from district to district. Reclamation charges full-cost water rates for landholders who irrigate land above the statutory acreage limitations, which are rates set to cover (1) the construction cost component associated with the project, plus interest; (2) actual operation and maintenance costs; and (3) any operation and maintenance deficits, if applicable.

ownership limits and are charged full-cost water rates on land irrigated in excess of the amount subject to the pricing limitations. Full-cost water rates include interest charges on the landholders' remaining allocated portion of construction costs and can be substantially higher than the subsidized rates charged for acres under the statutory pricing limitations.[35] For instance, officials in one irrigation district told us their full-cost water rates were roughly double and, in another district, about 30 times higher than the subsidized rates. Once irrigation districts or landholders have repaid their construction cost obligations in full—whether early, or as scheduled by the terms of their contract—the landholders are no longer subject to these acreage and pricing limitations. As a result, landholders may be able to receive project water, to the extent it is available, on additional land or at a subsidized rate once they have fulfilled their repayment obligations.

Reclamation officials told us that any foregone income in future years from full-cost water rates would reduce the return to the federal government associated with early repayment. According to Reclamation officials, the agency collected approximately $146.8 million from January 1988 through December 2013 in full-cost water rates from landholders who were irrigating land in excess of the amount subject to the statutory pricing limitations. Thus, if early repayment authority were exercised by those landholders, then the loss of full-cost water rate revenue in future years would at least partially offset the return to the government from early repayments. In addition, Reclamation officials and others we interviewed stated that early repayment would allow for the possibility of larger entities receiving project water at subsidized rates on larger landholdings sooner than intended under reclamation law—one of Reclamation's early goals in developing water projects throughout the western United States was to promote farming opportunities for small, family-owned operations. Other irrigation district officials told us, however, that even though their districts had landholders with excess acres who may be interested in early repayment, the elimination of acreage and pricing limitations would not likely serve as an incentive for the districts as a whole to repay early. For example, one official stated that her district would have to finance a loan to make early repayments on a lump-sum or

---

[35]Reclamation officials told us that the number of acres irrigated and the number of landholders that irrigate with project water under the full-cost rates fluctuates from year to year and from district to district, based on water availability and demand.

accelerated basis, which did not make sense compared with making annual, interest-free repayments under the terms of the contract.

Early Repayment Eliminates Reporting Requirements for Landholders

Early repayment also eliminates annual reporting requirements for landholders earlier than if repayment was made by the due date specified in the contract. Until their construction cost obligations are repaid, landholders are subject to annual reporting requirements to ensure landholders' compliance with acreage and pricing limitations. According to irrigation district officials and landholders we interviewed, completing these reports can be difficult and time-consuming for landholders and for districts, which must complete a form for Reclamation summarizing the reports submitted by landholders. For example, one landholder in Oregon said that it repaid its construction cost obligation early, after receiving statutory authority to do so in 2005, in part to eliminate the need to submit the annual reports. On the other hand, some irrigation district officials told us that while the reporting requirements were burdensome, eliminating the reporting requirements would not be a sufficient reason for the district to repay early, if granted the authority, without other incentives.

Early Repayment Potentially Provides Irrigation Districts with Greater Assurance of Project Water in Perpetuity

Early repayment potentially provides irrigation districts with a greater assurance of receiving available project water on a permanent basis. The right to water is generally determined by state law—which varies by state and can be complex—so repayment and water service contracts do not provide a right to water under state law. Under federal reclamation law, however, these contracts give irrigation districts assurance of a specified amount of water from the project's available water supply, which becomes permanent upon completion of repayment of the construction costs allocated to the districts.[36] Securing a permanent right to project water in a geographic area where water supply is uncertain was a key motivation in the Central Valley Project irrigation districts' desire to convert their contracts and repay their construction costs early, according to an attorney who represented those districts in pursuing and receiving such authority in 2009. In addition, for irrigation districts that receive and exercise authority to convert their water service contracts to repayment

---

[36]Contracts with Reclamation, however, do not provide a right to water under state law and delivery is contingent on the availability of water so districts may not necessarily receive water. For example, during the 2014 drought in California, Reclamation reduced the amount of water irrigation districts received. In addition, agency officials noted that the districts are still bound by all other provisions of a repayment contract, such as payment to Reclamation for operation and maintenance charges, once the construction cost repayment obligation is fulfilled.

contracts and repay early, the need for Reclamation and the districts to renegotiate water service contracts when they expire is eliminated, according to agency officials.[37] Reclamation officials and the attorney representing the Central Valley Project irrigation districts told us that renegotiating the terms of water service contracts can be time-consuming and unpredictable for landholders and their agricultural businesses and, therefore, repayment contracts may be preferable over water service contracts. On the other hand, the agency's flexibility for responding to water shortages, drought, and climate change-related issues could be limited as a result of fixing the amount of water an irrigation district receives under a repayment contract in perpetuity, according to a statement made by Reclamation's Commissioner in 2011.[38]

Conclusions

With population, agricultural production, and development in the West projected to continue to increase, Reclamation may be called upon to modify or expand existing capacity for water storage or delivery. In considering potential new work and affiliated funding arrangements, Congress, as well as water users and the public, may benefit from evaluating information on past water projects. In particular, Congress and others may want to assess information on how costs were allocated and how funding and repayment arrangements were established among various water users in the past. Reclamation compiles such information in the repayment statements it prepares annually for each water project with outstanding repayment obligations. However, Reclamation does not make it readily known to the public that this information is available upon request. By further disseminating information to the public that construction cost and repayment data are available, Reclamation may increase interested parties' opportunities to obtain cost and repayment information, and Reclamation would promote transparency and potentially

[37]Reclamation officials we interviewed indicated that a repayment contract is not technically needed for an irrigation district to repay its outstanding repayment obligations early and that early repayment could be authorized for a water service contract. If early repayment were authorized for a water service contract, then Reclamation would need to calculate a final repayment obligation and include provisions in the early repayment agreement that the irrigation district would be responsible for any future construction costs, according to Reclamation officials.

[38]Statement of Michael L. Connor, Commissioner, Bureau of Reclamation, U.S. Department of the Interior, before the Natural Resources Committee Subcommittee on Water and Power, U.S. House of Representatives, on H.R. 1837, San Joaquin Valley Water Reliability Act (Washington, D.C.: June 2, 2011).

increase informed participation by the public. This, in turn, could further enable Congress, water users, and the public to assess past funding arrangements and enhance their ability to make informed decisions for funding potential new work, such as to expand water storage capacity.

Recommendation for Executive Action

Consistent with Reclamation's policy to make construction cost repayment statements available to the public upon request, and to promote transparency and increase informed participation by Congress, water users, and the public, the Secretary of the Interior should direct Reclamation to better promote to the public that annual statements of project construction cost and repayment are available.

Agency Comments

We provided a draft of this report to the Department of the Interior for review and comment. On August 13, 2014, the department's audit liaison indicated in an e-mail that the department concurred with the recommendation and did not have any other comments.

As agreed with your offices, unless you publicly announce the contents of this report earlier, we plan no further distribution until 30 days from the report date. At that time, we will send copies of this report to the appropriate congressional committees, the Secretary of the Interior, and other interested parties. In addition, the report will be available at no charge on the GAO website at http://www.gao.gov.

If you or your staff members have any questions about this report, please contact me at (202) 512-3841 or morriss@gao.gov. Contact points for our Offices of Congressional Relations and Public Affairs may be found on the last page of this report. GAO staff who made major contributions to this report are listed in appendix V.

Steve D. Morris
Acting Director, Natural Resources and Environment

Appendix I: Objectives, Scope, and Methodology

This appendix provides information on the scope of our work and the methodology used for the following objectives: examine (1) the extent to which Reclamation collects and reports information on water project construction costs and the status of repayment by irrigation districts and (2) the extent to which irrigation districts can repay their allocated water project construction costs early and the implications of early repayment.

In conducting our work, we reviewed the Reclamation Act of 1902, the Reclamation Project Act of 1939, the Reclamation Reform Act of 1982, and other relevant laws. We reviewed Reclamation policies and directives and other Reclamation documents on water project construction cost allocation, repayment, and early repayment of construction costs. We also reviewed our July 1996 report on the status of construction cost allocations and repayments.[1] In addition, we conducted interviews with knowledgeable Reclamation officials at the agency's central office in Denver, Colorado, and all five regional offices (Great Plains, Lower Colorado, Mid-Pacific, Pacific Northwest, and Upper Colorado) about issues related to the status of repayment and early repayment. For our interviews with officials from each of the regional offices, we developed a set list of open-ended questions to obtain information and documentation on information they maintain on water project construction cost allocation and repayment information and the use and availability to the public of this information, as well as the opportunities for and potential implications of early repayment, among other things.

To determine the extent to which Reclamation collects and reports information on water project construction costs and the status of repayment by irrigation districts, we analyzed Reclamation's Statements of Project Construction Cost and Repayment (repayment statements) for fiscal year 2012, the most current data available at the time of our review. Reclamation provided repayment statements for 76 projects with outstanding repayment obligations with irrigation districts, and provided repayment statements for 43 of 54 projects with irrigation that no longer had outstanding obligations with irrigation districts (Reclamation policy calls for repayment statements to be prepared annually for all water projects with construction cost repayments outstanding. This policy does not apply to water projects where all water users, including irrigation districts, have repaid their construction cost allocations, and per

---

[1] GAO/RCED-96-109.

Reclamation policy, preparing repayment statements for these projects is optional). The data contained in repayment statements are generally tied to audited accounting records.[2] The repayment statements are prepared annually by the regional offices for each water project that has construction costs allocated to one or more water users with an outstanding repayment obligation. The repayment statements contain information on total costs for the water project, including construction costs incurred as of the end of the fiscal year; estimated future construction costs, and other costs that Reclamation includes in its repayment analysis for construction costs, such as capitalized operation and maintenance costs; the allocation of construction costs among project purposes, including irrigation; and the status of repayment for costs allocated to each project purpose, including repayment realized, anticipated future repayment, and any financial assistance granted to irrigation districts, such as credits, which relieve water users from a portion of their allocated repayment obligations. To analyze and interpret the data contained in the repayment statements, we relied, in part, on the relevant financial standards section on repayment statements in the Reclamation Manual, which provides guidance on the content and format for repayment statements. When the data in a repayment statement included estimated future construction costs, we subtracted these estimated costs from the projects' total costs because such costs have not yet been and, in some cases, may never be, incurred. To assess the reliability of Reclamation repayment data, we took steps such as reviewing the guidance for developing repayment statements in the Reclamation Manual; interviewing Reclamation officials from all five regional offices who were involved in preparing the repayment statements, as well as officials from Reclamation's central finance office in Denver; identifying the sources of data included in the repayment statements and the agency's review process; and following up with Reclamation officials to obtain clarifying information in instances where we identified discrepancies in the data. On the basis of these steps, we found the repayment statements to be sufficiently reliable for the purposes of this report.

We reviewed information from each of the five regional offices on the number of repayment and water service contracts in their respective

---

[2]We did not independently verify the accuracy of the audited financial reports that Reclamation used for the cost allocation and repayment obligation information contained in each project's repayment statements.

regions where irrigation districts were making repayments on their
allocated construction cost obligations, as of July 2014, for the Lower
Colorado, Mid-Pacific, Pacific Northwest and Upper Colorado regions
and, as of November 2013, for the Great Plains region. To assess the
reliability of the data provided by the regions concerning the number of
contracts of each type, we asked Reclamation officials a standard set of
questions concerning the reliability of the data and reviewed
corresponding documentation, and we found the data sufficiently reliable
for the purposes of our report. We also reviewed Reclamation's policies
and practices on making cost allocation and repayment information—
specifically, its repayment statements—available to the public, as well as
the Office of Management and Budget's open government directive and
associated documentation related to ensuring the transparency of
government information to the public.[3]

To examine the extent to which irrigation districts can repay their
allocated water project construction costs early, and the implications of
early repayment, we reviewed applicable laws, policies, and other
relevant documents. We also collected data from Reclamation's regional
offices on irrigation districts that have contractual or statutory authority to
repay early, districts that have exercised such authority, and the dates
and amounts of early repayments through December 2013. To assess the
reliability of the data provided by Reclamation concerning early
repayment, we asked Reclamation officials a standard set of questions
concerning the reliability of the data and reviewed corresponding
documentation, and we found the data sufficiently reliable for the
purposes of our report. In addition, we conducted legal research to
identify statutes that provide irrigation districts with the authority to repay
their construction cost obligations early. To help identify the implications
of early repayment, we reviewed the Reclamation Reform Act of 1982
and other laws and regulations that establish acreage and pricing
limitations and reporting requirements for landholders until their
repayment obligations are fulfilled. We also reviewed testimonies and a
statement for the record by Reclamation on draft legislation that would
have authorized early repayment for additional irrigation districts, and we
reviewed Congressional Budget Office cost estimates of various bills

[3]Office of Management and Budget, *Open Government Directive*, M-10-06 (Washington,
D.C.: Dec. 8, 2009); OMB Circular A-130, *Management of Federal Information Resources*
(Washington, D.C.: Nov. 28, 2000).

since 2005 that proposed expanding early repayment authority to certain irrigation districts.

For both objectives, we conducted interviews with officials from a nonprobability sample of eight irrigation districts and two landholders from five water projects located in California, Nebraska, Oregon, and Wyoming to collect information on the repayment of construction costs and related issues.[4] We selected these irrigation districts and landholders using criteria such as the type of contracts the districts held with Reclamation (repayment or water service contracts), their status of repayment, and whether or not the districts had early repayment authority. We also interviewed a nonprobability sample of nine individuals knowledgeable about Reclamation water projects on the status of repayments, early repayment authority, or both.[5] Using the "snowball sampling" technique, we identified these individuals by asking for referrals to others knowledgeable about Reclamation water projects and their repayment from others whom we had previously interviewed. Specifically, we interviewed staff from the Congressional Research Service and Congressional Budget Office, attorneys who have represented irrigation districts pursuing enactment of legislation authorizing early repayment, an attorney who has represented environmental organizations in litigation concerning Reclamation water projects, an environmental consultant, former congressional staff, and officials from the Family Farm Alliance and Taxpayers for Common Sense.

We conducted this performance audit from June 2013 to September 2014 in accordance with generally accepted government auditing standards. Those standards require that we plan and perform the audit to obtain sufficient, appropriate evidence to provide a reasonable basis for our findings and conclusions based on our audit objectives. We believe that the evidence obtained provides a reasonable basis for our findings and conclusions based on our audit objectives.

---

[4]Because we used a nonprobability sample, the information obtained in these interviews is not generalizable to other irrigation districts or landholders, but it provides illustrative information.

[5]Because we used a nonprobability sample, the information obtained in these interviews is not generalizable to other professionals knowledgeable about Reclamation water projects, but it provides illustrative information.

Appendix II: Cost Allocation and Repayment Information for 54 Projects for Which Irrigation Districts Have Fulfilled Obligations

The following two tables provide information on construction cost allocations by project purpose (table 3) and repayment status of construction costs allocated to irrigation (table 4) for 54 Bureau of Reclamation water projects for which irrigation districts have fulfilled their repayment obligations, as of the end of fiscal year 2012.

Table 3: Construction Cost Allocation by Project Purpose for 54 Bureau of Reclamation Water Projects for Which Irrigation Districts Have Fulfilled Their Repayment Obligations, as of the End of Fiscal Year 2012

Dollars in thousands

| | Construction costs[a] | | | | |
| | Reimbursable | | | | |
Region and project	Irrigation	Power	Municipal and industrial	Nonreimbursable[b]	Total[c]
Great Plains					
Angostura	$20,556	$346	$0	$8,908	$29,810
Colorado River	12,071	0	0	11,375	23,446
Fort Clark Unit	1,426	0	0	0	1,426
Glendo Unit	13,329	43,328	0	11,573	68,230
Heart Butte Unit	2,948	0	0	5,332	8,280
Intake	94	0	0	0	94
Kendrick	19,147	31,281	0	2,978	53,406
Lower Rio Grande, Mercedes Division	11,817	0	0	0	11,817
Lower Rio Grande, La Feria Division	5,774	0	0	0	5,774
Lower Yellowstone	6,281	0	0	36	6,317
Mirage Flats	3,102	0	0	112	3,214
Savage Unit	1,231	0	0	0	1,231
Sun River	19,104	0	0	9,764	28,868
W.C. Austin	10,613	0	1,080	3,426	15,119
Lower Colorado					
Boulder Canyon[d]					
Gila[d]					
Palo Verde Diversion Dam[d]					
Salt River[d]					
Yuma Auxiliary[d]					
Yuma[d]					
Mid-Pacific					
Humboldt	2,814	0	0	6,618	9,432
Santa Maria	9,586	0	0	2,068	11,654

Dollars in thousands

| | Construction costs[a] | | | | |
| | Reimbursable | | | | |
Region and project	Irrigation	Power	Municipal and industrial	Nonreimbursable[b]	Total[c]
Solano	35,505	0	5,274	10,050	**50,829**
Truckee Storage	1,643	33	0	0	**1,676**
Pacific Northwest					
Arnold[d]					
Avondale	573	0	0	0	**573**
Burnt River[d]					
Dalton Gardens	564	0	0	0	**564**
Frenchtown[d]					
Grants Pass	809	0	0	1,073	**1,881**
Lewiston Orchards	2,331	0	1,046	5,310	**8,687**
Little Wood River	1,053	0	0	1,418	**2,471**
Mann Creek	3,763	0	0	440	**4,203**
Missoula Valley[d]					
Okanogan	15,819	0	0	8,098	**23,918**
Palisades	29,963	35,511	0	34,807	**100,281**
Ririe[d]					
Spokane Valley	5,132	0	970	0	**6,102**
Wapinitia	509	0	0	1,154	**1,663**
Upper Colorado					
Balmorhea	437	0	0	0	**437**
Brantley	1,779	0	0	200,365	**202,144**
Carlsbad	11,584	0	0	1,220	**12,804**
Fruitgrowers Dam	2,262	0	0	0	**2,262**
Grand Valley	10,898	214	0	0	**11,112**
Middle Rio Grande	19,189	0	0	27,577	**46,766**
Moon Lake	1,801	0	0	0	**1,801**
Newton	755	0	0	2,454	**3,210**
Pine River	1,754	0	0	1,797	**3,551**
Rio Grande	27,301	17,592	0	4,090	**48,983**
Sanpete	434	0	0	0	**434**
Seedskadee	1,603	7,649	14,118	74,289	**97,658**
Strawberry Valley	11,589	0	0	17,998	**29,587**

Dollars in thousands

	Construction costs[a]				
	Reimbursable				
Region and project	Irrigation	Power	Municipal and industrial	Nonreimbursable[b]	Total[c]
Uncompahgre	18,401	0	0	0	**18,401**
Weber River	3,197	0	0	34	**3,231**
Total[c]	**$350,542**	**$135,953**	**$22,488**	**$454,364**	**$963,347**

Source: GAO analysis of Bureau of Reclamation data. | GAO-14-764

[a]The construction costs do not include any estimated future costs that Reclamation anticipates may occur to complete projects.

[b]Under reclamation law, nonreimbursable costs are those that are generally borne by the federal government because certain project purposes are viewed as being national in scope.

[c]Numbers may not sum to totals because of rounding.

[d]Statements of Project Construction Cost and Repayment were not available for these projects; per Reclamation policy, it is optional to prepare repayment statements for projects that do not have ongoing repayments.

Table 4: Repayment Status of Construction Costs Allocated to Irrigation for 54 Bureau of Reclamation Water Projects for Which Irrigation Districts Have Fulfilled Their Repayment Obligations, as of the End of Fiscal Year 2012

Dollars in thousands

	Construction costs allocated to irrigation[a]	Repayment of irrigation costs			Anticipated future repayment of costs allocated to irrigation	
Region and project	Irrigation	Irrigation districts[b]	Other repayment realized[c]	Credits[d]	Irrigation assistance[e]	Other[f]
Great Plains						
Angostura	$20,556	$718	$176	$0	$19,661	$0
Colorado River	12,071	3,799	0	8,272	0	0
Fort Clark Unit	1,426	72	12	4	1,338	0
Glendo Unit	13,329	814	5,716	0	6,799	0
Heart Butte Unit	2,948	145	1,470	10	1,323	0
Intake	94	47	0	43	0	4
Kendrick	19,147	750	4,776	0	11,533	2,088
Lower Rio Grande, Mercedes Division	11,817	8,110	23	3,684	0	0
Lower Rio Grande, La Feria Division	5,774	5,749	24	0	0	0
Lower Yellowstone	6,281	3,929	47	654	0	1,651
Mirage Flats	3,102	842	22	2,238	0	0
Savage Unit	1,231	144	231	0	857	0

Dollars in thousands

Region and project	Construction costs allocated to irrigation[a] Irrigation	Repayment of irrigation costs Irrigation districts[b]	Other repayment realized[c]	Credits[d]	Anticipated future repayment of costs allocated to irrigation Irrigation assistance[e]	Other[f]
Sun River	19,104	12,873	113	6,195	0	5
W.C. Austin	10,613	2,182	73	7,979	0	378
Lower Colorado						
Boulder Canyon[g]						
Gila[g]						
Palo Verde Diversion Dam[g]						
Salt River[g]						
Yuma Auxiliary[g]						
Yuma[g]						
Mid-Pacific						
Humboldt	2,814	2,976	0	0	49	0
Santa Maria	9,586	9,516	67	0	0	3
Solano	35,505	1,947	19,534	982	13,043	0
Truckee Storage	1,643	1,000	1	642	0	0
Pacific Northwest						
Arnold[g]						
Avondale	573	347	42	0	184	0
Burnt River[g]						
Dalton Gardens	564	356	0	0	208	0
Frenchtown[g]						
Grants Pass	809	809	0	0	0	0
Lewiston Orchards	2,331	2,101	230	0	0	0
Little Wood River	1,053	957	0	96	0	0
Mann Creek	3,763	811	2,952	0	0	0
Missoula Valley[g]						
Okanogan	15,819	4,246	95	11,478	0	0
Palisades	29,963	8,440	16,651	1,021	3,852	0
Ririe[g]						
Spokane Valley	5,132	2,667	50	0	2,358	57
Wapinitia	509	509	0	0	0	0
Upper Colorado						
Balmorhea	437	256	0	182	0	0

Dollars in thousands

Region and project	Construction costs allocated to irrigation[a] Irrigation	Repayment of irrigation costs Irrigation districts[b]	Other repayment realized[c]	Credits[d]	Anticipated future repayment of costs allocated to irrigation Irrigation assistance[e]	Other[f]
Brantley	1,779	1,247	1	532	0	0
Carlsbad	11,584	6,173	1,109	4,705	0	0
Fruitgrowers Dam	2,262	198	3	2,061	0	0
Grand Valley	10,898	5,844	72	4,982	0	0
Middle Rio Grande	19,189	15,709	0	3,506	0	0
Moon Lake	1,801	1,592	8	201	0	0
Newton	755	350	43	362	0	0
Pine River	1,754	1,334	75	348	0	0
Rio Grande	27,301	13,855	6,621	6,268	558	0
Sanpete	434	373	1	59	0	0
Seedskadee	1,603	0	411	0	1,192	0
Strawberry Valley	11,589	10,909	293	426	0	0
Uncompahgre	18,401	9,946	185	8,373	0	0
Weber River	3,197	3,185	31	0	0	0
Total[h]	$350,542	$147,827	$61,159	$75,301	$62,954	$4,186

Source: GAO analysis of Bureau of Reclamation data. | GAO-14-764

[a]Numbers may not sum to total because of rounding. In addition, construction cost allocation information does not include any estimated future costs to complete projects or any anticipated future repayment for those costs. Furthermore, an excess of repayment over costs is expected for the Brantley, Carlsbad, Humboldt, Middle Rio Grande, Pine River, Strawberry Valley, Sun River, Uncompahgre, and Weber River projects, so in some instances the repayment of irrigation costs, credits, and anticipated future repayment of costs allocated to irrigation may exceed the costs allocated to irrigation.

[b]Repayments that have been made pursuant to repayment, water service, or rehabilitation and betterment contracts, according to the Statements of Project Construction Cost and Repayment.

[c]Other repayments realized include contributions and revenues that Reclamation calls "incidental revenues," such as excess water sold to irrigation districts or revenue from land leased for grazing.

[d]Credits relieve water users from a portion of their allocated repayment obligations. Types of credits include congressionally authorized repayment reductions, or "charge-offs," and construction expenses determined to be nonreimbursable.

[e]Irrigation assistance is the amount of construction costs allocated to irrigation that the Secretary of the Interior determines that irrigation districts are unable to pay for a given project, which is repaid from other revenue sources, where available.

[f]Other anticipated future repayment includes repayment anticipated through future repayment contracts and contracts that have been deferred, among other things.

[g]Statements of Project Construction Cost and Repayment were not available for these projects; per Reclamation policy, it is optional to prepare repayment statements for projects that do not have ongoing repayments.

[h]Numbers may not sum to totals because of rounding.

Appendix III: Cost Allocation and Repayment Information for 76 Projects with Ongoing Repayments by Irrigation Districts

The following two tables provide information on construction cost allocations by project purpose (table 5) and repayment status of construction costs allocated to irrigation (table 6) for 76 Bureau of Reclamation water projects with ongoing repayments by irrigation districts, as of the end of fiscal year 2012.

Table 5: Construction Cost Allocation by Project Purpose for 76 Bureau of Reclamation Water Projects with Ongoing Repayments by Irrigation Districts, as of the End of Fiscal Year 2012

Dollars in thousands

| | Construction costs[a] | | | | |
| | Reimbursable | | | | |
Region and project	Irrigation	Power	Municipal and industrial	Nonreimbursable[b]	Total[c]
Great Plains					
Ainsworth Unit	$25,265	$0	$0	$1,378	$26,643
Almena Unit	6,270	0	368	14,872	21,510
Belle Fourche	72,925	0	0	8,556	81,482
Bostwick Division	68,767	0	0	39,495	108,262
Buffalo Rapids	5,264	0	0	0	5,264
Buford-Trenton	1,294	0	0	0	1,294
Colorado-Big Thompson	118,616	162,081	0	72,936	353,633
Crow Creek Unit	3,798	0	0	0	3,798
East Bench Unit	19,245	0	119	6,139	25,503
Frenchman-Cambridge Division	64,885	0	0	41,749	106,634
Fryingpan-Arkansas	75,321	151,356	167,572	217,780	612,029
Glen Elder Unit	4,068	0	263	53,246	57,577
Hanover-Bluff	9,534	0	0	0	9,534
Helena Valley Unit	17,347	0	1,025	995	19,367
Huntley	4,312	0	0	0	4,312
Keyhole Unit	3,713	0	0	4,942	8,655
Kirwin Unit	11,677	0	0	7,918	19,595
Milk River	15,004	0	96	3,569	18,669
North Loup Division	321,010	0	0	39,808	360,818
North Platte	33,268	16,222	0	7,769	57,258
Riverton Unit	76,157	1,059	0	787	78,003
San Angelo	17,057	0	6,643	68,273	91,973
Shoshone	38,753	7,025	10	461	46,250
Trinidad	6,436	0	0	0	6,436

Dollars in thousands

	Construction costs[a]				
	Reimbursable				
Region and project	Irrigation	Power	Municipal and industrial	Nonreimbursable[b]	Total[c]
Webster Unit	10,068	0	0	8,561	18,629
Lower Colorado					
Central Arizona[d]	1,155,069	606,616	1,231,980	1,401,053	4,394,717
Mid-Pacific					
Cachuma	28,145	0	26,479	45,394	100,017
Combined Projects	29,151	2,148	0	82,437	113,737
Central Valley	1,870,814	946,475	633,797	1,403,153	4,854,238
Lahontan Basin	20,233	3,445	0	67,104	90,782
Orland	12,898	0	0	28,431	41,329
Ventura River	22,146	0	18,265	56,406	96,818
Pacific Northwest					
Baker	5,475	0	0	3,909	9,384
Bitter Root	2,087	0	0	0	2,087
Boise	76,737	36,520	0	61,657	174,914
Chief Joseph Dam					
Foster Creek Division	4,115	0	0	18	4,132
Greater Wenatchee Division	8,664	0	0	745	9,410
Manson Unit	18,823	0	0	0	18,823
Whitestone-Coulee Unit	8,380	0	0	202	8,582
Columbia Basin	685,770	1,632,688	2,285	84,182	2,404,925
Crescent Lake Dam	3,827	0	0	0	3,827
Crooked River	12,152	0	0	38,360	50,512
Deschutes	18,749	0	25	31,843	50,616
Michaud Flats	5,009	0	0	252	5,262
Minidoka	62,781	96,466	0	177,584	336,831
Owyhee	20,873	0	0	217	21,090
Rathdrum Prairie	9,941	0	147	558	10,645
Rogue River Basin	17,850	14,892	0	6,926	39,668
The Dalles	6,824	0	0	26	6,850
Tualatin	31,540	0	4,713	20,592	56,845
Umatilla Basin	6,063	0	0	74,352	80,415
Vale	8,001	0	0	1,849	9,850
Yakima	149,420	14,857	0	122,206	286,483

Dollars in thousands

| | Construction costs[a] | | | | |
| | Reimbursable | | | | |
Region and project	Irrigation	Power	Municipal and industrial	Nonreimbursable[b]	Total[c]
Upper Colorado					
Bonneville Unit	359,249	145,665	1,175,631	1,019,704	2,700,249
Bostwick Park	6,656	0	0	3,843	10,499
Collbran	6,186	17,296	0	8,602	32,084
Dallas Creek	11,188	0	97,566	80,123	188,876
Dolores	365,268	36,372	15,244	163,508	580,392
Eden	13,916	0	0	84	14,000
Emery County	8,768	0	3,791	4,119	16,679
Florida	9,730	0	0	1,699	11,429
Fort Sumner	2,433	0	0	0	2,433
Hammond	7,215	0	0	225	7,439
Hyrum	3,299	0	0	1,954	5,253
Jensen Unit	5,763	0	46,916	17,595	70,274
Lyman	27,239	0	1,118	15,264	43,621
Mancos	5,144	0	0	0	5,144
Ogden River	20,574	0	0	6,588	27,162
Paonia	7,632	0	0	1,023	8,655
Preston Bench	690	0	0	0	690
Provo River	60,503	1,601	134,028	27,330	223,463
San Juan-Chama	28,800	0	38,966	15,827	83,594
Scofield	2,101	0	619	13,824	16,544
Silt	6,964	0	0	9,898	16,862
Smith Fork	4,300	0	0	5,478	9,777
Tucumcari	18,506	0	0	0	18,506
Vermejo[e]	2,340	0	0	253	2,593
Vernal Unit	11,030	0	716	9,311	21,056
Weber Basin	75,398	0	48,592	76,817	200,807
Total[f]	**$6,402,485**	**$3,892,785**	**$3,656,973**	**$5,791,759**	**$19,744,000**

Source: GAO analysis of Bureau of Reclamation data. | GAO-14-764

[a]The construction costs do not include any estimated future costs that Reclamation anticipates may occur to complete projects.

[b]Under reclamation law, nonreimbursable costs are those that are generally borne by the federal government because certain project purposes are viewed as being national in scope.

[c]Numbers may not sum to totals because of rounding.

[d]The Arizona Water Settlements Act, the Arizona Water Settlement Agreement, which the act ratified, and a stipulated judgment that ended multiyear litigation fixed allocation of the project's water and repayment obligations without regard to specific water uses such as irrigation, which is a typical practice. The amounts reflected in the Central Arizona Project Statement of Project Construction Cost and Repayment for specific project purposes are inferred based on assumptions made by Reclamation officials. *See* Arizona Water Settlements Act, Pub. L. No. 108-451, tit. I, 118 Stat. 3478 (2004), the Arizona Water Settlement Agreement, and *Cent. Ariz. Water Conservation Dist. v. United States*, No. CIV 95-625, No. CIV 95-1720.

[e]Cost allocation and repayment information for Vermejo was last updated in 2007 because, since that time, repayment of the projects has been indefinitely deferred.

[f]Numbers may not sum to totals because of rounding. Also, these figures do not include construction cost allocation information for one water project that provides irrigation, the Klamath project in the Mid-Pacific region. Reclamation has not prepared a final repayment statement for this project since fiscal year 2001 because it is in the process of crediting revenues from leasing land, among other things, according to Reclamation officials According to a draft repayment statement prepared for the Klamath project for fiscal year 2010, the total cost of the project was $121.9 million, of which $101.2 million in costs were allocated to irrigation, and $20.7 million were allocated to nonreimbursable purposes.

Table 6: Repayment Status of Construction Costs Allocated to Irrigation for 76 Bureau of Reclamation Water Projects with Ongoing Repayments by Irrigation Districts, as of the End of Fiscal Year 2012

Dollars in thousands

Region and project	Construction costs allocated to irrigation[a] Irrigation	Repayment of irrigation costs Irrigation districts[b]	Other repayments realized[c]	Credits[d]	Anticipated future repayment of costs allocated to irrigation Irrigation districts[b]	Irrigation assistance[e]	Other[f]
Great Plains							
Ainsworth Unit	$25,265	$6,007	$305	$0	$4,159	$14,794	$0
Almena Unit	6,270	519	60	0	392	5,304	-5
Belle Fourche	72,925	5,487	4,196	2,375	2,795	57,503	570
Bostwick Division	68,767	16,119	1,385	0	7,285	43,977	0
Buffalo Rapids	5,264	1,332	39	3,846	47	0	0
Buford-Trenton	1,294	35	115	402	552	0	190
Colorado-Big Thompson	118,616	29,942	10,432	1,969	677	75,525	71
Crow Creek Unit	3,798	143	72	0	8	3,577	0
East Bench Unit	19,245	1,557	1,813	0	187	15,688	0
Frenchman-Cambridge Division	64,885	8,544	-360	2,682	2,345	51,675	0
Fryingpan-Arkansas	75,321	158	0	0	74,191	972	0
Glen Elder Unit	4,068	0	1,294	0	8	2,766	0
Hanover-Bluff	9,534	1,272	204	26	258	7,774	0

Dollars in thousands

Region and project	Construction costs allocated to irrigation[a] Irrigation	Repayment of irrigation costs Irrigation districts[b]	Other repayments realized[c]	Credits[d]	Anticipated future repayment of costs allocated to irrigation Irrigation districts[b]	Irrigation assistance[e]	Other[f]
Helena Valley Unit	17,347	857	368	94	57	15,971	0
Huntley	4,312	1,740	168	410	152	0	1,843
Keyhole Unit	3,713	219	370	0	140	2,985	0
Kirwin Unit	11,677	1,318	449	0	537	9,373	0
Milk River	15,004	8,348	1,331	3,375	899	0	1,050
North Loup Division	321,010	10,502	391	0	24,135	285,982	0
North Platte	33,268	24,345	2,643	3,299	923	825	1,232
Riverton Unit	76,157	5,052	5,121	17,502	2,946	45,113	422
San Angelo	17,057	13,507	24	224	3,302	0	0
Shoshone	38,753	15,536	1,541	11,705	9,708	433	415
Trinidad	6,436	1,761	0	0	4,675	0	0
Webster Unit	10,068	949	159	0	551	8,408	0
Lower Colorado							
Central Arizona[g]	1,155,069	60,477	42,759	848,876	202,957[h]	0	0
Mid-Pacific							
Cachuma	28,145	3,938	16,731	0	3,484	0	3,991
Combined Projects	29,151	28,358	777	0	16	0	0
Central Valley	1,870,814	729,568	73,290	16,695	829,230	47,026	175,004
Lahontan Basin	20,233	4,946	2,045	4,578	166	0	8,498
Orland	12,898	3,489	279	0	0	0	9,129
Ventura River	22,146	17,973	388	0	2,027	0	1,758
Pacific Northwest							
Baker	5,475	969	7	52	383	4,065	0
Bitter Root	2,087	2,071	7	2	7	0	0
Boise	76,737	33,782	31,169	90	8,449	0	3,248
Chief Joseph Dam							
Foster Creek Division	4,115	1,165	10	743	208	1,799	189
Greater Wenatchee Division	8,664	3,689	23	0	988	3,964	0

Dollars in thousands

Region and project	Construction costs allocated to irrigation[a] Irrigation	Repayment of irrigation costs Irrigation districts[b]	Other repayments realized[c]	Credits[d]	Anticipated future repayment of costs allocated to irrigation Irrigation districts[b]	Irrigation assistance[e]	Other[f]
Manson Unit	18,823	1,330	0	0	1,330	16,163	0
Whitestone-Coulee Unit	8,380	561	0	0	349	7,470	0
Columbia Basin	685,770	59,205	68,370	0	13,661	494,327	50,208
Crescent Lake Dam	3,827	3,789	0	30	0	0	8
Crooked River	12,152	3,633	870	296	1,909	3,552	1,892
Deschutes	18,749	7,282	403	1,700	9,364	0	-1
Michaud Flats	5,009	2,557	31	0	341	2,081	0
Minidoka	62,781	41,757	11,662	178	1,810	0	7,373
Owyhee	20,873	10,678	282	0	9,913	0	0
Rathdrum Prairie	9,941	2,004	1,860	174	62	5,840	0
Rogue River Basin	17,850	5,727	158	9	2,296	9,660	0
The Dalles	6,824	1,744	70	0	806	4,204	0
Tualatin	31,540	2,881	15	0	2,993	25,316	335
Umatilla Basin	6,063	1,863	977	2,289	935	0	0
Vale	8,001	5,468	200	412	1,921	0	0
Yakima	149,420	61,808	9,553	56,023	4,998	13,652	3,387
Upper Colorado							
Bonneville Unit	359,249	1,271	629	62,129	6,266	280,116	8,839
Bostwick Park	6,656	734	92	0	347	5,483	0
Collbran	6,186	1,004	5,097	0	85	0	0
Dallas Creek	11,188	4,810	186	0	1,456	4,736	0
Dolores	365,268	5,021	487	0	19,022	335,293	5,445
Eden	13,916	935	123	0	381	12,478	0
Emery County	8,768	1,960	26	0	389	6,393	0
Florida	9,730	1,456	138	0	320	7,692	125
Fort Sumner	2,433	1,807	42	0	602	0	23
Hammond	7,215	356	42	0	180	6,637	0
Hyrum	3,299	2,644	12	107	536	0	0
Jensen Unit	5,763	420	9	0	330	5,005	0
Lyman	27,239	1,651	60	0	1,802	23,727	0

Dollars in thousands

Region and project	Construction costs allocated to irrigation[a] Irrigation	Repayment of irrigation costs Irrigation districts[b]	Other repayments realized[c]	Credits[d]	Anticipated future repayment of costs allocated to irrigation Irrigation districts[b]	Irrigation assistance[e]	Other[f]
Mancos	5,144	870	3	4,169	103	0	0
Ogden River	20,574	13,735	159	504	6,241	0	0
Paonia	7,632	1,365	142	0	955	5,170	0
Preston Bench	690	582	0	0	108	0	0
Provo River	60,503	6,871	49,775	137	4,129	0	0
San Juan-Chama	28,800	3,515	429	0	70	24,686	100
Scofield	2,101	1,291	8	32	769	0	0
Silt	6,964	787	33	0	173	5,971	0
Smith Fork	4,300	923	81	0	103	3,194	0
Tucumcari	18,506	4,878	18	11,816	1,795	0	0
Vermejo[i]	2,340	43	0	232	2,065	0	0
Vernal Unit	11,030	1,381	81	0	959	8,608	0
Weber Basin	75,398	35,065	84	12,299	27,950	0	0
Total[i]	$6,402,485	$1,353,332	$351,812	$1,071,483	$1,318,668	$2,022,948	$285,340

Source: GAO analysis of Bureau of Reclamation data. | GAO-14-764

[a]Numbers may not sum to totals because of rounding. In addition, construction cost allocation information does not include any estimated future costs to complete projects or any anticipated future repayment for those costs. For the Upper Colorado region, anticipated future repayment as reported assumes that the Bonneville Unit and Mancos projects will be completed. Furthermore, an excess of repayment over costs is expected for the Fort Sumner, Ogden River, Provo River, and Shoshone projects, so in some instances the repayment of irrigation costs, credits, and anticipated future repayment of costs allocated to irrigation will exceed the costs allocated to irrigation.

[b]Amounts include repayments that have been made or are anticipated pursuant to repayment or water service contracts, as well as some repayments made through rehabilitation and betterment contracts, according to the Statements of Project Construction Cost and Repayment.

[c]Other repayments realized include contributions and revenues that Reclamation calls "incidental revenues," such as excess water sold to irrigation districts or revenue from land leased for grazing.

[d]Credits relieve water users from a portion of their allocated repayment obligations. Types of credits include congressionally authorized repayment reductions, or "charge-offs," and construction expenses determined to be nonreimbursable.

[e]Irrigation assistance is the amount of construction costs allocated to irrigation that the Secretary of the Interior determines that irrigation districts are unable to pay for a given project, which is repaid from other revenue sources, where available.

[f]Other anticipated future repayment includes repayment anticipated through future repayment contracts and contracts that have been deferred, among other things.

[g]The Arizona Water Settlements Act, the Arizona Water Settlement Agreement, which the act ratified, and a stipulated judgment that ended multiyear litigation fixed allocation of the project's water and repayment obligations without regard to specific water uses such as irrigation, which is the typical practice. The amounts reflected in the Central Arizona Project repayment statement for specific project purposes are inferred based on assumptions made by Reclamation officials. *See* Arizona Water Settlements Act, Pub. L. No. 108-451, tit. I, 118 Stat. 3478 (2004), the Arizona Water

Settlement Agreement, and *Cent. Ariz. Water Conservation Dist. v. United States*, No. CIV 95-625, No. CIV 95-1720.

[h]This $203.0 million in anticipated future repayment for the Central Arizona Project is being repaid, pursuant to federal law, a settlement agreement, and stipulated judgment, by a municipal corporation that operates and maintains the Central Arizona Project. The United States had entered into repayment contracts with irrigation districts for the repayment of Central Arizona Project irrigation distribution system construction costs. Under the Central Arizona Project Settlement Act of 2004 and the Arizona Water Settlement Agreement, however, irrigation districts that voluntarily relinquished Central Arizona Project water to which they were entitled by the terms of their contracts received relief from their repayment obligations, among other things.

[i]Repayment information for Vermejo was last updated in 2007 because, since that time, repayment of the projects has been indefinitely deferred.

[j]Numbers may not sum to totals because of rounding. Also, these figures do not include repayment information for one water project that provides irrigation, the Klamath project in the Mid-Pacific region. Reclamation has not prepared a final repayment statement for this project since fiscal year 2001 because it is in the process of crediting revenues from leasing land, among other things, according to Reclamation officials. According to a draft repayment statement prepared for the Klamath project for fiscal year 2010, $101.2 million in costs were allocated to irrigation, $9.0 million was repaid by irrigation districts, $46.2 million was repaid from other sources, and $33.1 million was provided in financial assistance.

The following two tables provide information on irrigation districts with contractual authority for landholders to repay their outstanding construction cost obligations early, and early repayments made (table 7) and irrigation districts with statutory authority for the districts or landholders to repay their outstanding construction cost obligations early, and early repayments made (table 8), as of December 2013.

Table 7: Irrigation Districts with Contractual Authority for Landholders to Repay Outstanding Construction Cost Obligations Early, and Early Repayments Made, as of December 2013

Region and project	Irrigation districts with contractual authority for early repayment by landholders	Irrigation districts in which the district or landholders repaid early[a]	Early repayments made
Great Plains			
North Platte	2	2	$15,637,349
Huntley	1	1	unavailable[b]
Pacific Northwest			
Boise	1	1	62,282
Deschutes	1	1	199,703
Michaud Flats	1	1	94,924
Minidoka	1	0	0
Minidoka and Palisades[c]	40	25	418,056
Owhyee	3	3	622,614
Rogue River Basin	1	1	380,048
Umatilla Basin	1	1	9,406
Yakima	3	3	1,242,022
Total	**55**	**39**	**$18,666,403**[d,e]

Source: GAO analysis of Bureau of Reclamation data. | GAO-14-764

[a]In most of the 39 irrigation districts with landholders who exercised their contractual early repayment authority, all of the landholders repaid early, and therefore the districts as a whole repaid early.

[b]According to Reclamation data, 487 landholders in this irrigation district repaid their construction cost obligations early, from 1940 through 2000, but Reclamation could not readily provide the amounts of those early repayments.

[c]According to Reclamation officials, these irrigation districts have contractual authority for landholders within their districts to repay their construction cost obligations early for two projects, Minidoka and Palisades.

[d]Numbers may not sum to total because of rounding.

[e]Total does not include early repayments for the Huntley project.

Table 8: Irrigation Districts with Statutory Authority for the Districts or Landholders to Repay Outstanding Construction Cost Obligations Early, and Early Repayments Made, as of December 2013

Region and project	Irrigation districts with statutory authority for early repayment	Statute and terms of early repayment authority	Early repayments made
Great Plains			
Pick-Sloan Missouri Basin Program[a]	2	Pub. L. No. 106-366 (2000) - authorized transfer of title to certain Reclamation assets to the Farwell Irrigation District and Sargent Irrigation District, which had repayment contracts, in exchange for approximately $2.8 million. According to Reclamation officials, this amount was an accelerated repayment that was discounted from the districts' outstanding repayment obligations.	$2,847,360
Mid Pacific			
Central Valley	24	Pub. L. No. 111-11, § 10010 (2009) – (1) directed Reclamation to convert 19 irrigation districts' water service contracts to repayment contracts by December 31, 2010, and (2) authorized Reclamation to convert the water service contracts of 5 other irrigation districts upon those districts' request.[b]	200,072,648
		Required the converted contracts to require early repayment, either in lump-sum or accelerated prepayment, by specified time frames.	
		Discounted the early repayment of outstanding construction costs by half the 20-year Treasury rate.	
		Required districts to repay construction costs and other capitalized costs properly assignable to them after completion of construction on the Central Valley Project and a final cost allocation by Reclamation.	
		Prohibited the use of power revenues to aid in repayment of construction costs allocated to irrigation.	
Central Valley	1	Pub. L. No. 106-377, appx. B, tit. II, § 212 (2000) – authorized transfer of title to the project's Sly Park Unit to the El Dorado Irrigation District, in exchange for $11.5 million to relieve repayment obligations and extinguish all debts associated with the district's contracts.	11,500,000[c]
Central Valley	1	Pub. L. No. 106-566, tit. V, § 503 (2000) - authorized transfer of title to certain facilities to the Foresthill Public Utility District, in exchange for approximately $2.7 million, which relieved the irrigation district of all repayment obligations for the facilities, and relieved the district of all debt under the district's water service contract.	2,772,221[d]
Pacific Northwest			
Minidoka	1	Pub. L. No. 110-229, § 508 (2008) - authorizes landholders in the A&B Irrigation District to repay at any time the project's construction costs allocated to their land.	639,783

Region and project	Irrigation districts with statutory authority for early repayment	Statute and terms of early repayment authority	Early repayments made
Rogue River Basin	2	Pub. L. No. 109-138 (2005) - authorizes landholders in the Medford Irrigation District and the Rogue River Valley Irrigation District to repay at any time the construction costs of the project facilities allocated to their land.	78,513
Upper Colorado			
San Juan-Chama	1	Pub. L. No. 107-20, § 2402 (2001) - requires Reclamation to accept prepayment for all remaining repayment obligations under a specific contract if early repayment is offered by the Middle Rio Grande Conservancy District.	2,329,091
Total	**32[e]**		**$220,239,616**

Source: GAO analysis of Bureau of Reclamation data and laws. | GAO-14-764

[a]The Pick-Sloan Missouri Basin Program contains multiple Reclamation water projects.

[b]The San Joaquin River Restoration Settlement Act (Pub. L. No. 111-11, tit. X, subtit. A, pt. I, § 10010(a)(2) (2009)) did not specify the irrigation districts within the Friant Division for which Reclamation was authorized (but not required) to convert the district's water service contract to a repayment contract upon the district's request. However, according to Reclamation officials, there were five such irrigation districts at that time.

[c]According to Reclamation officials, the El Dorado Irrigation District had four repayment and water service contracts, which provided the district with water for irrigation as well as municipal and industrial purposes. The agency could not readily provide the early repayment amounts specifically for irrigation.

[d]According to Reclamation officials, the Foresthill Public Utility District had a water service contract that provided the district with water for irrigation as well as municipal and industrial purposes. Of the $2.7 million the district repaid early, $194,085 was for its irrigation construction cost obligation.

[e]Of the 32 irrigation districts with statutory authority for the districts—or, in some cases, landholders within those districts—to repay their construction cost obligations early, 30 districts either repaid early as a whole or had some landholders who repaid early. Two irrigation districts in the Central Valley Project that were authorized to repay early by Pub. L. No.111-11, § 10010(a) (2009) did not repay early; according to Reclamation officials, one of those districts had no outstanding repayment obligation, and the other district chose not to exercise its authority.

Appendix V: GAO Contact and Staff Acknowledgments

GAO Contact	Steve D. Morris, (202) 512-3841 or morriss@gao.gov
Staff Acknowledgments	In addition to the individual named above, Alyssa M. Hundrup (Assistant Director), Josey Ballenger, Marya Link, and Jeanette Soares made key contributions to this report. Stephen Brown, Cindy Gilbert, Paul Kinney, and Alison O'Neill also provided assistance.

www.ingramcontent.com/pod-product-compliance
Lightning Source LLC
Chambersburg PA
CBHW080553290526
45790CB00006B/2642